CITIES OF THE
WORLD

BEIJING

BY DEBORAH KENT

CHILDREN'S PRESS®
A Division of Grolier Publishing
New York London Hong Kong Sydney
Danbury, Connecticut

CONSULTANTS

Guy Alitto, Ph.D.
Professor of History
Professor of East Asian Language & Civilization
University of Chicago

Linda Cornwell
Learning Resource Consultant
Indiana Department of Education

Project Editor: Downing Publishing Services
Design Director: Karen Kohn & Associates, Ltd.
Photo Researcher: Jan Izzo
Pronunciations: Courtesy of Xue Ying Fung, Chinese teacher; former student, Guangzhou Foreign Language Institute, Guangzhou (Canton), China

---

NOTES ON CHINESE PRONUNCIATION

Chinese does not really have stress the way English does. Instead, it has tones on each syllable. Tones are pitch changes. In English, pitch changes are used to show the difference between a question ("oh?") and an answer ("oh."), as well as other things. The tones are very important in Chinese. If the wrong tone is used, a completely different word has been spoken. However, to simplify, we are not including tones in this book. The best way to learn to pronounce tones is to practice with a native Chinese person. For pronunciations, *GH* is always like g in get; *DZ* is pronounced as in gad*z*ooks. The vowels are *EE* as in feet, *IH* as in bit, *AY* as in day, *EH* as in bet, *AH* as in father, *AW* as in draw, *OH* as in toe, *OOH* as in book, *OO* as in boot, *IGH* as in high, *OW* or *AOW* as in cow, and *UH* as the *a* in about. *ING* and *ONG* are as in sing and song.

Library of Congress Cataloging-in-Publication Data

Kent, Deborah.
    Beijing / by Deborah Kent.
        p. cm. — (Cities of the world)
    Includes index.
    Summary: Describes physical aspects, history, and social life and customs of the capital of the People's Republic of China.
    ISBN 0-516-20023-2
    1. Peking (China)—Juvenile literature. [1. Peking (China)]
I. Title II. Series: Cities of the world (New York, N.Y.)
DS795.K46 1996   96-5951
951'.156—dc20   CIP

TABLE OF CONTENTS

P E A C E

On October 1, 1949, a vast crowd gathered before the great northern gate to Beijing's central square. The gate is a magnificent structure 100 feet high. It has turrets, balconies, and a two-story yellow-tiled roof. To the people of Beijing, it is known as the Tiananmen Gate, the Gate of Heavenly Peace.

Beijing (BAY-ZHING)
Tiananmen (TEE-EHN-AHN-MUHN)

The Tiananmen Gate led from the square into Beijing's Forbidden City. For hundreds of years, the Forbidden City was the home of China's imperial family. Behind its moats and walls, the emperor and his court enjoyed a life of luxury. Beyond the gates, most Chinese people lived in desperate poverty.

In the square, the crowd shifted restlessly. At last, the long-awaited moment arrived. A man stepped onto the gate's main balcony and delivered a passionate speech. The speaker's name was Mao Zedong. He announced the creation of a new nation, the People's Republic of China.

China is one of the most ancient countries in the world. For nearly 3,000 years, it was ruled by a series of emperors. During the twentieth century, China underwent enormous changes. An uprising in 1911 ended the imperial way of life. Through the decades that followed, warring factions vied for control. Finally, Mao Zedong emerged as a powerful new leader. Mao led a revolution that transformed China forever.

Mao Zedong was the head, or chairman, of China's Communist Party. The Communists took over China in 1949. They promised to erase the differences between rich and poor. They called for all Chinese people to work as equals in forging a splendid new nation. Chairman Mao sought to turn China from a land of struggling farmers to a modern industrial country. He urged the Chinese people to stride forward, casting aside the chains of the past.

Tiananmen Square and the Gate of Heavenly Peace

A portrait of Mao Zedong hangs on the Gate of Heavenly Peace.

Mao Zedong (MAOW ZUH-DOHNG)

This gilded statue of a lion is one of a pair that guard the entrance to the Forbidden City.

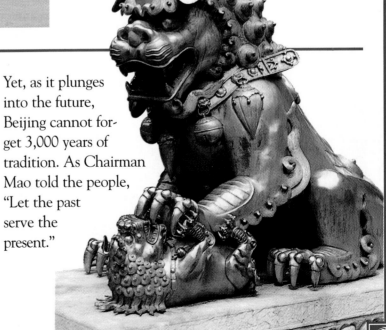

From the Gate of Heavenly Peace, Chairman Mao gazed across a rippling sea of people. They packed the central square that is now known as Tiananmen. Tiananmen Square lies at the very heart of the city of Beijing, capital of the immense land of China. It belongs to the people. It is a meeting place, a place for games and kites and political rallies. To the north, beyond the Tiananmen Gate, stand the gleaming palaces of the old Forbidden City. Though the emperors are gone, the past still clings to Beijing, and to all of China.

Few cities on earth are as old as Beijing. Seldom has any city changed so much in so short a time.

Yet, as it plunges into the future, Beijing cannot forget 3,000 years of tradition. As Chairman Mao told the people, "Let the past serve the present."

THE PEOPLE OF BEIJING

The roar of bulldozers and the pounding of hammers can be heard everywhere in Beijing. Beijing is a city under construction. Workers are constantly tearing down old buildings to put up offices, apartments, and factories.

Most Beijing residents prefer to live in the new apartment buildings. But many old houses still survive along a network of back alleys called *hutongs*. Usually, three or four of these tiny houses are clustered around a shared courtyard. The court-yard houses of Beijing are a legacy of the days before the revolution.

hutong (HOO-TONG)

HOME AND HEARTH

The walls and light poles near Beijing bus stops are often plastered with notices. People post these handwritten signs much as Americans place classified ads in newspapers. Some signs announce items for sale. Others are placed by people who want to change jobs. Many notices are posted by people who need apartments.

Apartments in Beijing are very inexpensive. The problem with apartment hunting is not the cost, but the shortage of places to live. The population of Beijing has grown tremendously over the past 50 years. It climbed from 2 million in 1949 to nearly 10 million by the late 1990s. Despite endless construction projects, the city does not have enough apartments to go around. The people of Beijing are accustomed to very crowded living conditions. Privacy is a luxury to treasure.

By American standards, a modern apartment in Beijing is anything but fancy. Often the elevators do not work. There is seldom much furniture, and there may be no hot water. Many people do not have such appliances as washing machines or vacuum cleaners. They wash their clothes by hand and sweep their floors with brooms made of twigs.

Among the millions of residents of Beijing are this woman and her grandchild.

Students at Beijing University reading wall posters

A Beijing apartment offers elegant living compared with a courtyard house. Courtyard houses crowd the hutongs that thread back and forth behind the main streets. Few of these homes are equipped with gas stoves or running water. During Beijing's icy winters, people in the courtyard houses burn balls of coal dust mixed with tar and mud. Year-round, they get their water from a tap in the courtyard. Their toilets are outdoor latrines. Despite these hardships, many people brighten their courtyards by planting gardens. Sunflowers can often be seen swaying above a courtyard wall.

GETTING FROM HERE TO THERE

When a couple marries in China, the groom traditionally gives his bride three gifts. They are sometimes called "the gifts of the four wheels." These wedding presents are a watch, a sewing machine, and a bicycle.

More people own automobiles than ever before in Beijing. But a car is still beyond the budget of many families. All over the city, people ride bicycles to work, to school, and on errands. Millions of bicycles jam the streets. They swerve past pedestrians and zigzag among buses, cars, trolleys, and taxis. At major intersections, the police try to direct traffic. They wave red batons and shout orders over loudspeakers. Their efforts only add to the noise and confusion.

Beijing opened its first subway line in 1965. The subways are fast and clean, but their routes are limited. Buses, on the other hand, go to every corner of the city. At each stop, people push to climb aboard while others fight to get off.

Many children in Beijing ride in bicycle sidecars like this one.

Some Beijing policemen stand on platforms as they direct traffic.

注意安全

注意安全

Bicycle riders in Beijing

Passengers pack the aisles, wedged between bags and boxes. Bus fares are very low. Yet the overworked conductor can seldom collect a fare from everyone. Some passengers simply can't shove their way to the fare box. Others purposely avoid having to pay. Bus rides often turn into high drama, with the conductor shouting at a fare dodger while the other passengers take sides.

Trucks are increasingly common on Beijing streets.

But wagons drawn by mules or horses still haul many goods to market. Some peddlers lead donkeys through the hutongs. The animals are loaded with squash, peppers, and other produce. In transportation, as in everything else, Beijing has not completely shed the old ways.

THE HIGHER PATH

A stranger cannot help getting lost in the hutongs of Beijing. The alleys twist this way and that, blocked by gates and walls. Following an ancient tradition, each courtyard house along the hutongs is protected by a "ghost wall," a barricade just before the entrance. According to Chinese superstition, ghosts can move forward only in a straight line. Thus, they cannot enter a house if they have to turn right or left around a wall to reach the door.

The children sitting on the steps in front of a temple (right) might live in one of the traditional Beijing courtyard houses shown below.

Ethnic Diversity in Beijing

China is home to more than fifty ethnic minorities. About 200,000 Hui people live in Beijing. The Hui are followers of Islam, a faith most widespread in the Arab nations. Some Hui women veil their faces when they go out on the streets of Beijing. This practice is in keeping with strict Islamic teachings.

Until the Communist revolution, the people of China followed a complex set of superstitions and religious beliefs. They lived in a world of ghosts, gods, and demons who must constantly be appeased. The ghosts of ancestors played a crucial role in the people's lives. These ghosts brought health and prosperity if they were happy. If they were displeased, they could bring bad luck.

In addition to the superstitions of the common people, China had three major religions: Confucianism, Daoism, and Buddhism.

Confucianism is based on the teachings of the scholar Kongfuzi. Most Westerners (Europeans and Americans) know him as Confucius. Confucius taught that each person should carry out his or her particular duties in life.

Children should respect their parents. Wives should obey their husbands. Parents should teach and protect their children. And the emperor should rule with firmness and wisdom.

Daoism is based on the work of an ancient scholar, Laozi. Laozi's teachings encourage people to live in harmony with nature.

Confucianism (CON-FYOO-SHUHN-IH-ZUHM)
Daoism (DOW-IH-ZUHM)
Buddhism (BOO-DIH-ZUHM)
Kongfuzi (KONG FOO-DZUH)
Laozi (LOW-DZUH)
Hui (HWAY)
Islam (IHZ-LAHM)

The third Chinese religion, Buddhism, arrived from India in about the second century A.D. Buddhists believe that the soul is reborn many times on its way to spiritual perfection. Most people try to find happiness by buying things and seeking pleasure. Buddhists reject this idea. Only by putting aside the things of this world can the soul reach a state of true happiness.

To this day, many Buddhist temples stand in Beijing. They are filled with sculptures showing scenes from Buddhist mythology. Smiling statues of Buddha, the religion's great teacher, welcome followers of the faith. Guanyin, the goddess of mercy, holds out gifts in her many arms. Under the Communists, most of these temples have been turned into museums. They are no longer places of worship.

The Temple of Buddhist Virtue

A Buddhist monk in Beijing

Guanyin (GWAHN-YEEN)

16

When the Communists came to power in 1949, they claimed that religion and superstition helped to keep the Chinese people in poverty. In Beijing and throughout China, they tried to stamp out religious practices. In a sense, communism replaced the earlier traditions. It is sometimes said that communism is China's fourth religion.

Through the Communist revolution, China underwent a sweeping transformation. Perhaps no other nation in history has ever changed so swiftly and

dramatically. With more than 1 billion people, China is the most heavily populated country on earth. Beijing is the capital of this vast and complex nation. It stands at the very center of the whirlwind of change.

In the Temple of Heaven (left), Ming and Qing emperors prayed to heaven for a good harvest.

CAPITAL

In 1967, an obscure clerk died in Beijing. The world paid little attention to his passing. His death, however, marked the end of an era that stretched back more than 2,000 years. Puyi, the humble Beijing clerk, had once sat on the Dragon Throne in the Imperial Palace. He was the last emperor of China.

Puyi (POO-YEE)

BEWARE THE BARBARIANS!

Most cities spring up along rivers or a seacoast. But Ji, the first city on the site of present-day Beijing, was not built on a major waterway. It arose 100 miles from the sea, at the edge of China's northern plain. Ji was founded in the eighth century B.C. as a trading center and military outpost. It controlled two key mountain passes to the northwest. The city welcomed merchants and their caravans. Its soldiers guarded the passes against invaders.

Qin Shihuangdi, the first Qin emperor, is shown here on his throne.

The plains to the north and west of Beijing were the home of many nomadic tribes. From time to time, these steppe dwellers swept down on the city. The people of Ji regarded these northern enemies as "barbarians."

For centuries, the land that is now China was broken into many separate states. In 221 B.C., a powerful military leader called Qin Shihuangdi gathered these states under his rule. He proclaimed himself the founder of the Qin Dynasty, or ruling family. Qin Shihuangdi made Ji the capital of his empire. To keep the northern tribes at bay, he connected several frontier fortifications to form a barricade. This barricade became the Great Wall of China.

The View from Space

From a satellite orbiting the earth, only one human-made object is visible. That structure is the Great Wall of China. The Great Wall is the largest construction project ever completed by human beings. When it was finished, sometime during the fifteenth century A.D., it stretched some 1,500 miles across northern China. In most places, the wall stood 30 feet high. It was dotted every 200 yards with 40-foot watchtowers. Today, much of the wall has crumbled. Several large sections still stand firm, however, including a portion just north of Beijing.

Ji (JEE)
Qin Shihuangdi (SHEEN SHEE-HWANG-DEE)

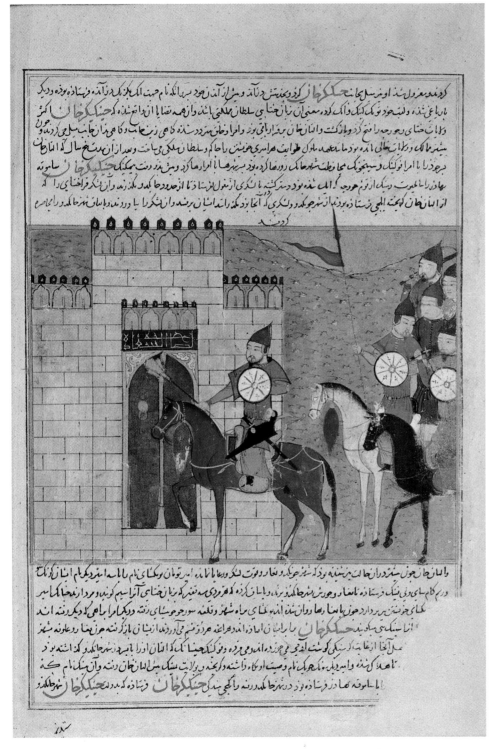

For more than 2,000 years, one dynasty followed another. As ruling families rose and fell, the city of Ji was often renamed. For a time, it was called Youzhou. Later, it was known as Dadu, and later still, Beiping. At last, during the Ming Dynasty (1368-1644), it was named Beijing (or Peking, according to an earlier spelling). In Chinese, the name means "Northern Capital."

Through most of their long history, the people of Beijing dreaded the coming of barbarians from the north and west.

This depiction of Mongols taking over a Chinese town was taken from a fourteenth-century manuscript on the history of the Mongols.

Youzhou (YOH-JOH)
Dadu (DAH-DOO)
Beiping (BAY-PING)
Ming (MING)
Mongol (MAHN-GUHL)
Genghis Khan (GHEHN-GHISS KAHN)

Genghis Khan (left and above) was the cruel leader of the Mongol warriors who took over Beijing in the year 1215.

In 1215, the worst fears of the people of Beijing were realized. Hordes of Mongol warriors on horseback broke through the Great Wall and swarmed into the city. Their leader, Genghis Khan, was a man of unspeakable cruelty. He once declared that the greatest joy in life was "to conquer one's enemies, to seize their property, to see their families in tears, to ride their horses, and to possess their daughters and wives." Murdering, burning, and looting, the Mongols took over the capital city of Beijing. Genghis Khan must have been in his glory.

THE SONS OF HEAVEN

On the site where Ji once stood, a splendid new city arose. It was built by Genghis Khan's grandson, Kublai Khan. In 1275, an Italian merchant named Marco Polo visited Dadu, Kublai Khan's "great capital." He marveled at its magnificent gateways and palaces and its throngs of people. He admired its traders with their jewels, silks, and spices. "The streets are so straight and wide that you can see right along from end to end and from one gate to another," he wrote. "The whole city is arranged like a chessboard."

Actors from the show Marco Polo *(right) perform at the Palace Museum in Beijing.*

Kublai Khan built a beautiful new city called Dadu on the site of Ji.

This colored miniature drawing shows Marco Polo being received by Kublai Khan.

As Marco Polo noted, Kublai Khan had laid out his city in a neat, gridlike pattern. That pattern survives today in most of central Beijing. City blocks still resemble a chessboard's even squares.

In 1403, a Ming Dynasty emperor called Yongle redesigned the central portion of the city. Behind moats and high stone walls he built the Forbidden City. It was a complex of ornate halls and palaces for members of the imperial court and their servants. No man except the emperor was permitted to spend the night there.

Behind the walls of the Forbidden City lived the emperor, the Son of Heaven. When he was hungry, the finest chefs in the land prepared exotic delicacies. If he was bored, dancers, jugglers, and acrobats rushed to entertain him. If he was tired, musicians lulled him to sleep with gentle melodies.

Kublai Khan (KOO-BLUH KAHN)
Yongle (YONG-LOOH)

CHINESE CONJURING EXTRAORDINARY.

Conjurers were among those who entertained Marco Polo when he was a guest of Kublai Khan.

The emperor bore an enormous responsibility for the welfare of the kingdom. On special occasions throughout the year, he carried out vital ceremonies. By fulfilling his ceremonial duties, the Chinese believed that the emperor ensured good harvests and victory in war.

On ceremonial occasions, the emperor mounted the gilded Dragon Throne. This throne, adorned with twisting bronze dragons, stood in the Hall of Supreme Harmony within the Forbidden City. Incense burned in beautifully painted urns. Gongs and chimes filled the air with sound. As courtiers and officials approached the throne, they kowtowed before the Son of

The Dragon Throne in the Hall of Supreme Harmony

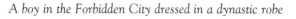

A boy in the Forbidden City dressed in a dynastic robe

Heaven. In the kowtow, a person expressed humility by kneeling and touching the forehead to the floor nine times.

kowtow (KOW-TOW)

The imperial court enjoyed every imaginable luxury. Beyond the gates of the Forbidden City, however, the common people struggled to survive. Sheltered behind his walls, the emperor had little knowledge of the world outside.

The beautifully decorated interior of the Temple of Heaven

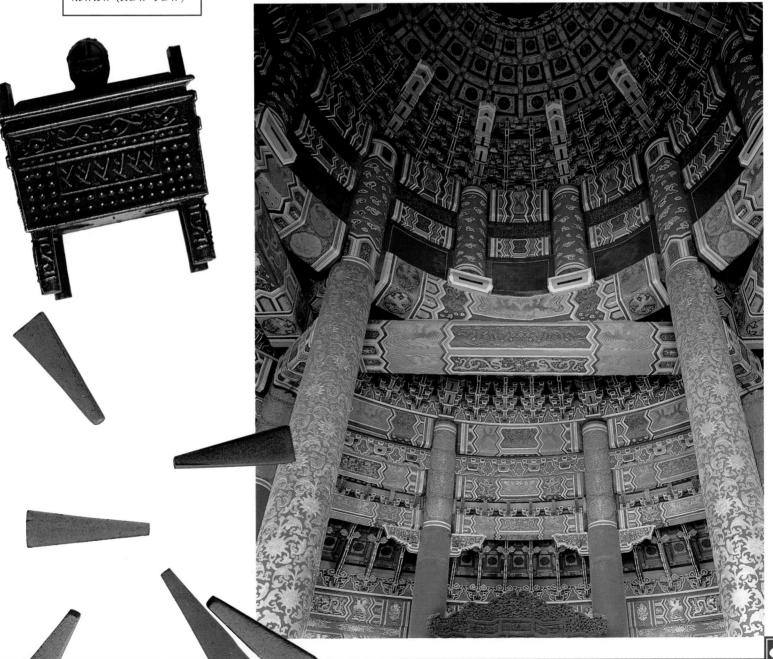

Cixi, the Empress Dowager (1835-1908)

During most of China's history, women had few opportunities to advance. But for almost fifty years, the Empress Dowager Cixi was the most influential person in the land. As the mother of a child emperor, she gained tremendous power. Cixi held her position through a series of clever intrigues. She undermined efforts to reform China's weak and corrupt government. Cixi's actions helped to set the stage for Sun Yatsen's 1911 revolution.

Chinese war junks being destroyed by the British in 1841

Like the emperor, China itself seemed to exist behind walls. The Chinese were proud of their ancient civilization and its achievements. They saw no need for foreign goods or strange new ideas from across the seas. China could not remain isolated forever, however. During the nineteenth century, it was drawn into warfare with the British, and then with the Japanese. These wars weakened the last imperial dynasty, the Qing, which toppled in 1911. An American-educated leader named Sun Yatsen established China's first democratic government. His government did not last long. Military leaders called warlords scrambled for power.

In 1931, Japan invaded China's northeastern province of Manchuria.

Sun Yatsen

Cixi (TSEE-SHYEE)
Sun Yatsen (SOOHN YEE-SHEE-EHN)
Qing (CHEENG)
Manchuria (MAN-CHU-REE-UH)
Jiang Jieshi (JEE-AHNG JEE-EH-SHEE)

During World War II, Japanese troops were in control of most of eastern China.

Six years later, Chinese and Japanese troops fought a bloody battle on Beijing's Marco Polo Bridge. Japanese forces surged into the capital. Throughout World War II, Beijing was under Japanese rule. The Japanese occupation was a time of hunger and hardship.

At last, in 1945, the war ended with Japan's defeat. The Japanese withdrew from Beijing, leaving the city in chaos. Most people were living in desperate poverty. Furthermore, China was still wracked by war. Chinese Communists fought the forces of General Jiang Jieshi (Chiang Kaishek), who had the support of the United States. The future of the nation hung in the balance.

"CHINA HAS ARISEN!"

In 1949, the Communists drove Chiang Kaishek out of mainland China to the island of Taiwan. On October 1, Mao Zedong proclaimed the founding of a new Communist nation, the People's Republic of China. From the Gate of Heavenly Peace, he told a vast, cheering crowd, "China has arisen!"

During the 1950s, the Communists set out to create a new, modern nation. In Beijing, they cleared slums and built high-rise apartments. They opened schools and established literacy programs for adults. New factories began producing steel, machinery, and other goods.

Even children were expected to work for the nation's improvement. All over China, girls and boys were given fly swatters. Every week, each child brought a box of dead flies to a neighborhood official. The child who killed the most flies won a special prize.

Taiwan (TIGH-WAHN)

Left: An armed-forces honor guard in Beijing

Above: During the Cultural Revolution, members of the Red Guard removed street signs with traditional Chinese names. The streets were later given such names as "Anti-Revisionist Street."

Beijing schoolchildren in class

In 1966, Mao launched a movement that he claimed would strengthen the nation. He said that many people still clung to old ideas and old ways. Such people felt superior to others because of their education or their possessions. They failed to give the revolution their total support.

Mao tried to wipe away every trace of the old ways. Teachers and doctors were no longer members of a privileged class. They were sent to work like peasants in the fields. Bands of teens, known as the Red Guard, destroyed symbols of imperial China. They burned books and works of art. They even tore down ancient buildings. Millions of lives were lost or ruined during this turbulent decade, which is known as the Cultural Revolution.

Chairman Mao Zedong (right) proclaimed the founding of the People's Republic of China on October 1, 1949.

In China, white is the color of mourning. In September 1976, white-clad mourners filled the streets of Beijing. Mao Zedong was dead. In the years that followed, Mao's successors gradually allowed the Chinese people to have greater personal freedom. Most people in Beijing looked back on the Cultural Revolution as a catastrophe.

In the spring of 1989, thousands of students gathered in Tiananmen Square for a series of massive demonstrations. The students asked for a change in government policy. They wanted to move toward democracy. Eventually, the army was called in to control the crowd. On June 4, troops fired on the protesters. No one knows how many young people lost their lives.

Members of the Red Guard mourning the death of Chairman Mao Zedong during a mass memorial service

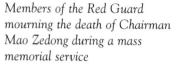

A brave and determined student faces down government tanks during the 1989 demonstration in favor of democracy.

Pro-democracy students hold an open-air news conference during the 1989 demonstrations.

Red flags flying in Tiananmen Square

Most estimates range in the hundreds.

Beijing has changed in ways that Mao Zedong could never have imagined. But it is still the capital of a Communist nation. The Communist system blends with the traditions of ancient China to determine how people live in Beijing.

Weekends do not exist in Beijing. People work six days out of every seven. Days off are staggered throughout the week. Saturdays and Sundays are not special. In Beijing, every day is a working day.

Perhaps because the people of Beijing work so hard, they throw themselves joyfully into recreation. They love sports, theater, and other entertainments. Holidays are a delight for everyone, young and old.

UP AND MOVING

Every morning at sunrise, the streets of Beijing suddenly fill with people. On each block, schoolchildren, workers, and senior citizens line up. They bend and stretch their bodies in a series of graceful exercises. They are performing *tai-jiquan,* or "ultimate supreme boxing." Tai-jiquan developed about 300 years ago as a system of self-defense. Today, it is chiefly a method for keeping in shape. The complete routine involves 128 balletlike positions. It can be carried out in about fifteen minutes.

For the people of Beijing, athletics is part of everyday life. Schools, factories, and neighborhoods sponsor a variety of sports teams. In one form or another, soccer has been played in China for more than 1,000 years. Today, the capital is dotted with soccer fields for amateur teams. Major-league soccer teams compete at the

Morning tai-jiquan excercises in a Beijing park

A tai-jiquan master practicing his art

| *tai-jiquan* (TIGH-JEE-CHWAHN) |

Beijing Workers' Stadium, which seats 80,000 spectators. The Chinese are considered the most civilized soccer players in the world. They do not fight or hurl insults on the field. A popular slogan is, "Friendship first, competition second."

Basketball and volleyball are also popular in Beijing. Table tennis, or Ping-Pong, reached China during the 1950s and became very popular. Most parks and recreation centers have Ping-Pong tables. Instead of a woven net, these tables have an upright slab of concrete down the center.

In addition to team sports, the people of Beijing enjoy gymnastics, track and field, and swimming. Many parks and recreation centers have pools.

Swimming became immensely popular in the 1960s after Mao Zedong took a televised swim in the Yangtze River.

Yangtze (YANG-SEE)

Children and their teacher in a Chinese dance class

Children are involved in many organized activities after school. But they still find time to play on their own. Girls play a form of hop-scotch, marking off squares on the sidewalk. Boys often play with wooden tops. By striking them with sticks or whips, they make the tops spin at dizzying speeds.

The climate of Beijing is somewhat like that of New York City. Winters are cold, and summers are hot and humid. Outdoor fun changes with the seasons. In the winter months, people bundle up in quilted coats to go ice-skating. They also ride over the crusted snow on homemade ski boards. Because Beijing is very flat, downhill

Two girls on a class trip play a hand-clapping game.

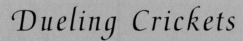

Dueling Crickets

Many Chinese shops sell tiny cages made of wire or bamboo. These cages are designed for captive crickets. Some people keep crickets to enjoy their chirping. Children often catch them to watch them fight. Some adults also like cricket fights, placing bets on their favorites. The most serious followers of the sport match opponents according to size, weighing them on tiny scales.

skiing is almost unknown. People squat on their ski boards, pushing themselves along with sticks.

During the summer, families flock to Beijing's parks. They splash in the pools, row boats on the lakes, and have picnics under the trees. On any summer day, the sky is alive with sailing kites. The Chinese have been building kites for thousands of years.

Today's kites are works of art and imagination. Some are tiny, and others measure up to 16 feet in length. Kites may look like birds, fish, ships, or dragons. A skillful handler can turn kite-flying into a dazzling performance. Kites can swoop and soar and twist and plunge like a living creature doing acrobatics in the sky.

Boating on Kunming Lake, at the Summer Palace

SHOW TIME

During the 1990s, the price of a television set dropped in Beijing. For the first time, television became part of everyday life. In addition to Chinese programs, the people of Beijing watch many shows from the United States. Though fascinated with TV, they also enjoy more traditional forms of entertainment. The opera, the theater, and the circus provide fun for everyone.

In Beijing, opera is a stunning spectacle of costumes, makeup, singing, dance, and acrobatics. In some productions, emperors, generals, and beautiful maidens prance across the stage in imperial splendor. In more modern operas, young women and men struggle with evil landowners and other enemies of the revolution. The colors used in a character's makeup and costume speak to the audience like a secret code. Red stands for bravery. Blue means wildness and rebellion. Black represents goodness and strength, while white can be read as treachery.

This elaborately costumed singer is performing in a production of the popular Beijing Opera.

Many Beijing theaters offer comedy acts. Comic duos perform humorous skits full of slapstick gags. Their antics are similar to those of Laurel and Hardy, Abbott and Costello, and other Western comedy teams.

Circus performers were looked down upon in imperial China. They were seen as untrustworthy vagabonds, little better than beggars. After the revolution, however, the Chinese government recognized the circus as a form of folk art. Today, the government encourages young gymnasts, mimes, and jugglers to develop their talents. The Beijing Circus is an extravaganza of tumblers and high-wire artists, clowns and animal acts.

Among the most amazing performers are the stilt walkers. They cavort about on towering stilts 12 feet high, looking like giant grasshoppers. Their flawless balance comes from years of devoted practice.

This acrobat is doing an amazing balancing act at the Cultural Show in Beijing.

Chinese opera stars

41

THE HOLIDAY SPIRIT

When it snows in Beijing, people pour into the streets, carrying brooms. Like a well-trained army, they sweep the city clean. When there is work to be done, everyone is expected to help. But at *Xin Nian Jie* (New Year, or Spring Festival), duties are tossed aside. For three days, the people revel in noise, confusion, food, and fun.

Officially, China follows the Western calendar, beginning the year on January 1. The people of China, however, still follow the ancient lunar calendar, which is based on the phases of the moon. The lunar calendar varies somewhat from year to year. The new year begins sometime between January 21 and February 19, whenever the new moon appears.

In the days before Xin Nian Jie, trains and buses are more packed than usual. People from the countryside pour into Beijing to spend the holiday with relatives in the city. City dwellers rush to join their families in distant provinces. Everyone is going home for the most important holiday of the year.

Below and page 43: Participants in a colorful New Year parade

Xin Nian Jie
(SHEEN NEE-EHN JEE-EH)

New Year is a time for casting out the refuse of the past. To ensure that the coming year will be a lucky one, only cheerful words must be spoken. Each family prepares a series of delicious meals with special holiday dishes. Everyone turns out to watch fireworks displays and processions. Children wait eagerly for the lion dancers, who lead the final parade. Several performers work inside an enormous lion costume. With perfectly timed movements, they make the lion walk, crouch, and spring.

Xin Nian Jie is a celebration of renewal. A very different holiday is *Qing Ming,* or the Feast of Pure Brightness, held during the first week in April. Qing Ming is a holiday to honor the dead. People visit the cemeteries and clear weeds from the graves of their ancestors. Then the party begins. Food baskets are opened, tablecloths are spread on the ground, and everyone enjoys a picnic. Afterward, there is always time for flying kites.

Qing Ming (CHEEN MING)

Another traditional holiday in Beijing is the Mid-Autumn Feast, or *Zhongqiu Jie*. It is a quiet, reflective time of thanksgiving. In the evening, people gather in courtyards to drink tea and gaze at the moon. The moon is a symbol of unity and harmony. Round pastries called mooncakes are a special treat at this time of year. Mooncakes are usually filled with a paste made from lotus seeds.

Spectacular fireworks are displayed on National Day, October 1.

44

Drummers in bright costumes at the Spring Festival

This boy seems to be enjoying what he is hearing on his radio.

Since the revolution, the people of Beijing have celebrated several new holidays. May 1 is International Workers' Day, honoring working men and women around the world. It is celebrated with picnics, dancing, and fireworks. National Day, October 1, commemorates the day Mao Zedong announced the formation of the People's Republic of China. Workers and schoolchildren march in parades, and officials make political speeches. Whatever its purpose, each holiday gives people a chance to break away from rules and schedules. They gather with friends in celebration.

Since 1949, Beijing has seen astonishing growth. The city spread farther and farther, devouring the surrounding countryside. Within the central city, streets were widened. Old houses disappeared to make way for apartments and factories. Drab but practical new buildings replaced ancient walls, gates, and arches. In its rush to modernize, it sometimes seems that Beijing has erased its past. But here and there, relics of imperial China are carefully preserved. Beijing embraces the future, but it cannot forget where it has been.

THE OUTER FRINGES

Beijing is a city of factories. The southern portion of the capital bristles with smokestacks. Sprawling apartment complexes house millions of families. Most apartment buildings are bleak, gray structures, faceless and unadorned. They meet basic needs, with nothing wasted on frills.

Practical necessity controls even Beijing funerals. Land is needed for farms, highways, and housing. There is little room for cemeteries. Today, most people are cremated when they die.

In contrast, the Ming emperors of old were buried in splendor. The Valley of the Ming Tombs lies 30 miles north of Beijing. It is reached by a 4-mile avenue called the Great Spirit Way. The avenue is lined with statues of horses, camels, elephants, warriors, and creatures from Buddhist mythology. Within a walled complex are the tombs of thirteen Ming emperors. The final resting place of Yongle, founder of the Forbidden City, is a vast burial mound some 100 feet high.

One of the gates on the grounds of the Ming Tombs

This stone figure of a horse is one of the many sculptures lining the Great Spirit Way, the 4-mile avenue leading to the Ming Tombs.

This marble replica of a Mississippi River steamboat stands in the lake at Empress Cixi's Summer Palace.

A young tourist poses on the grounds of the Summer Palace.

The Summer Palace of Empress Cixi is another example of imperial excess. The empress created the palace with funds intended to rebuild the Chinese fleet. The palace grounds include groves, gardens, and a large artificial lake. Within the lake stands the marble replica of a Mississippi River steamboat, built on the Empress's whim. The empress's theater is now a museum where attendants wear elaborate costumes from the Qing Dynasty. Cixi's jewelry, cosmetic cases, and other possessions are on display.

The Temple of Heaven stands in southeastern Beijing. It was built in 1420. Each fall, the emperor made a pilgrimage to this temple to pray for a good harvest. Any disaster to the crops was a sign that the emperor was out of favor with the gods. The harvest ritual was last carried out in the early 1900s.

DOWNTOWN BEIJING

Central Beijing is the oldest part of the city. With the renovations that have taken place since the revolution, little of the ancient city remains. Downtown Beijing has many new landmarks. One is the 17-story Beijing Hotel, the capital's tallest building. The biggest department store in the city is known as the Hundred Goods Emporium. It sells toys, appliances, and a variety of other goods not found in most smaller shops.

Parks offer a welcome retreat from the congestion of downtown Beijing. Coal Hill Park surrounds a human-made hill north of the Forbidden City. Evil spirits were once thought to come from the north. The hill was created to protect the emperor's palace from ghosts and demons. At one end of the park stands the Hall of the Emperor's Long Life, now a recreation center for children. Sun Yatsen Park is west of Tiananmen Square. It was named for the leader of the 1911 revolution that overthrew the last imperial dynasty.

A *pavilion at Coal Hill Park*

Old friends rest and enjoy a chat in a Beijing park.

Everyone who visits the Beijing Zoo is captivated by the playful giant pandas.

Early evening light helps to make this scenic view of Behai Park a perfect subject for a painting.

In the center of the park stands a square altar built by the Emperor Yongle in 1421. A complex of sixteenth-century Buddhist temples also stands within the park. Now the Workers' Palace of Culture, it is used as a college and recreation center. Purple Bamboo Park is a forest of bamboo trees. It is threaded with walkways for leisurely strolling. Nearby is the Beijing Zoo. The zoo's most prized exhibit is a group of endangered giant pandas.

The Temple of the Source of Buddhist Teaching is one of the oldest buildings in Beijing. Erected to honor soldiers killed in battle, it was completed in A.D. 696.

Though traditional Buddhism has faded in modern China, this temple is still in use. Buddhist monks are trained at a school on its grounds.

At the heart of Beijing spreads Tiananmen Square, the Square of Heavenly Peace. Greatly expanded since the revolution, it covers 123 acres. On ordinary days, Tiananmen Square is a place for people to meet, relax, and enjoy being outdoors. It can also be the scene of huge political rallies. Paving stones in the square are numbered to help marshals organize columns of marchers. From the center of the square soars a 124-foot monument to the heroes of the revolution. The base of the monument is carved with scenes from Chinese history from 1840 to 1949.

On the western edge of Tiananmen Square stands the Great Hall of the People. It houses many departments of government and serves as the parliament building. Its chandeliered entrance hall is 100 yards long. Across the square from the Great Hall is the Museum of Chinese History. Exhibits include bones and tools from China's earliest inhabitants. They date back nearly half a million years. There are precious paintings on silk, carvings in jade and ivory, and delicate porcelain vases. The museum emphasizes the sufferings of the Chinese people under

There is more than enough room in enormous Tiananmen Square to accommodate bicyclists by the hundreds (above) and school events such as the one pictured at the left.

Singing Birds

Among the most interesting places to visit in Beijing are the city's bird markets. The markets sell many kinds of birds from all over China. Beijing families often keep songbirds as pets. On sunny days, they take their caged birds to the park for a taste of fresh air. Sadly, many Chinese songbirds are becoming rare. In part, this is due to the practice of taking baby birds from their nests to sell them as pets.

the emperors and foreign invaders. The Chinese Art Museum is another museum on the square. Its fourteen galleries display paintings and sculptures by Chinese and foreign artists. This museum gives visitors a chance to watch artists at work.

The body of Mao Zedong lies in a crystal coffin within a towering mausoleum in Tiananmen Square. The entrance hall to the mausoleum is adorned with a statue of Chairman Mao. A splendid tapestry depicts China's rivers and mountains. One hall contains copies of Mao's many writings.

This sculpture (left) in front of the Mao Zedong Mausoleum (above) depicts what the Communists called "Socialist Realism."

THE FORBIDDEN CITY

In the days of the Ming and Qing Dynasties, no man but the emperor was permitted to pass the night within the Forbidden City. The Forbidden City was a 250-acre complex of palaces, halls, and temples. It nestled behind walls and moats north of Tiananmen Square. Today, the gates stand open and the complex is forbidden no longer. The public is welcome to explore what remains of the imperial palaces.

A Chinese philosopher once wrote, "The emperor stands at the center of the earth and stabilizes the people within the four seas." The center of the emperor's power was the Dragon Throne. It stood in the Hall of Supreme Harmony in the Forbidden City. The emperor reached the throne by mounting a special ramp, carved from a 250-ton block of marble. Today, visitors file past the Dragon Throne, awed to imagine the solemn ceremonies that once took place in this regal chamber. In the neighboring Hall of Perfect Harmony, the emperor's gilded *palanquin* is on display. The palanquin is a canopied litter in which the emperor rode, carried by servants.

Beyond the Hall of Supreme Harmony, the Forbidden City is a maze of gardens, courtyards, and palaces. In the Palace of Earthly Tranquility, animals were sacrificed during religious rituals. The Hall of the Care of the Heart was the Empress Cixi's living quarters.

Within the walls of the Forbidden City

54

Tourists at the Forbidden City

palanquin (PAH-LUHN-KEEN)
Wumen (WOO-MUHN)

A woman in traditional dress

In one hall, visitors can gaze at the imperial treasures. Glass cases display exquisite porcelains, carvings, and pictures made of precious stones.

Many of the servants who lived in the Forbidden City rarely had a chance to step outside. The Imperial Gardens offered their only glimpse of flowers and greenery. The gardens are a lovely expanse of wooded hills, pools, and bamboo groves. Once the domain of royalty, they are now an oasis of peace for the hardworking citizens of Beijing.

The grandest entrance to the Forbidden City is the Wumen Gate, which stands 125 feet high. Its great U-shaped base is adorned with five pavilions. Yet it is the Tiananmen Gate, the Gate of Heavenly Peace, that especially draws visitors. From this gate, Mao Zedong declared the most sweeping revolution in history. Leading from the walled Forbidden City to the vast Tiananmen Square, the gate is a symbol of change. It speaks of an ancient land that set out bravely to become a new nation.

FAMOUS LANDMARKS

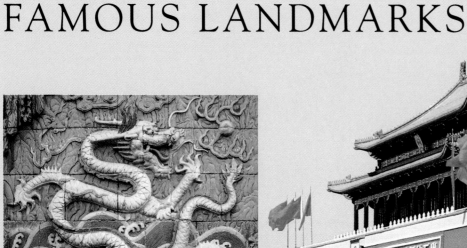

This dragon relief appears on the Imperial Palace

The Gate of Heavenly Peace at Tiananmen Square

Tiananman Square
Covering 123 acres, Tiananmen Square is the largest city square in the world. At the center stands a 124-foot monument to the heroes of the 1949 revolution. The square is often used for political rallies.

Palace Museum
Many buildings of Beijing's Forbidden City, once home to the emperors of the Ming and Qing Dynasties, are open to the public. In the Hall of Supreme Harmony stands the Dragon Throne, where the emperor sat on ceremonial occasions. On display in several halls are clothing, furniture, and other relics of imperial splendor.

Great Hall of the People
Located on the western edge of Tiananmen Square, the Great Hall houses many government bureaus and serves as China's parliament building.

Museum of Chinese History
This museum traces the history of China from ancient times to the present. It contains art objects, archaeological exhibits, and relics from China's many imperial dynasties.

Museum of the Revolution
Adjoining the Museum of Chinese History, this museum covers the rise of the Communist Party in China and the story of the 1949 revolution.

Temple of Heaven
The emperors of China used to visit this Buddhist temple every fall to pray for a good harvest. It is a fine example of the architecture of the Ming Dynasty. The temple stands in a 675-acre park.

Behai Park
This popular park west of the Forbidden City has a striking white pagoda that once served as a Daoist shrine. A museum in the park displays stone tablets with ancient Chinese writings.

Huge portraits of Russian Communist leaders Joseph Stalin and V. I. Lenin outside the Great Hall of the People

Right: The Temple of Heaven

This white pagoda at Behai Park was once a Daoist shrine.

Purple Bamboo Park

Ten distinct species of bamboo grow in this park. Children love the playground section, with its swings, slides, and assorted monkey bars. Students gather in the English Quarter to practice speaking English to one another. Any English-speaking foreigner is a very welcome attraction.

Hall of Ancient Astronomy

This museum stands on the site of an observatory built in 1279. It houses sixteen early instruments used for observing the stars and measuring the move-ments of heavenly bodies. These instruments were brought to China in the sixteenth and seventeenth centuries by European traders and missionaries.

Bell and Drum Tower

The first tower on this site was built in the reign of Kublai Khan. The tower once held twenty-four enormous drums, one of which still survives today. The drums were struck thirteen times each evening to signal the closing of the city gates. The tower's bells rang each morning to announce the start of a new day.

Valley of the Ming Tombs

A broad avenue called the Great Spirit Way leads to this complex of tombs northwest of Beijing. The valley contains the splendid tombs of thirteen rulers of the Ming Dynasty. The most spectacular is that of Yongle, who founded the Forbidden City.

Summer Palace of Cixi

This elaborate palace outside Beijing was a getaway for Cixi, the Empress Dowager. To build the palace, Cixi used funds allotted to the Chinese navy. The only ship ever built with the money is the marble replica of a Mississippi steamboat in the palace's artificial lake.

Beijing University

More than 10,000 students study on this quiet, tree-shaded campus. Many come from developing countries in Africa and Asia. The university was founded in 1898, when China was struggling to absorb new ideas from the outside world.

FAST FACTS

POPULATION

Beijing:	7.5 million
Metro Area:	9.5 million

AREA   151 square miles

CLIMATE   Beijing has hot, humid summers, with an average July temperature of 79 degrees Fahrenheit. Winters are bitter cold, though there is little snow. The average January temperature is minus 24 degrees Fahrenheit. During April and May, Beijing is often swept by dust storms from the Gobi Desert to the north. Clouds of dust cover the city, filtering into houses and getting into people's clothes. Most rainfall occurs during the summer months.

INDUSTRIES   Beijing is one of China's major manufacturing centers. Factories produce chemicals, machinery, furniture, and processed foods. In addition, craftspeople in small workshops make porcelain, tapestries, and ceramic tiles.

NEIGHBORHOODS   Central Beijing is laid out in a gridlike pattern. The Forbidden City is a 250-acre complex of palaces, halls, and gardens bordering Tiananmen Square. It is now a museum. Chang'an Avenue, crossing the city south of the square, is a major street of shops and businesses. Extensive renovation has obliterated many old neighborhoods. In some sections, small courtyard houses still cluster along alleys behind main streets. Manufacturing is most heavily concentrated in the southern part of the city.

CHRONOLOGY

8th century B.C.
The city of Ji is founded on the site of present-day Beijing

221 B.C.
Qin Shihuangdi unites much of present-day China

A.D. 1215
Mongols led by Genghis Khan invade the city, causing tremendous destruction

1275
Marco Polo visits Dadu, the newly rebuilt city on the site of present-day Beijing

1368
The Ming Dynasty is founded, beginning one of the greatest eras in Chinese culture

1644
Manchurians from the northeast conquer China and found the Qing Dynasty

1842
China is defeated by the British in the Opium War, a conflict over trading rights

1895
China is defeated by the Japanese naval fleet in the Sino-Japanese War

1898
Cixi, the Empress Dowager, moves into her newly constructed Summer Palace

1911
Sun Yatsen overthrows the Qing Dynasty and establishes a democratic government

1931
Japan invades Manchuria in northeastern China

Schoolchildren in costumes

1937
Japan defeats Chinese troops at the Marco Polo Bridge and occupies Beijing

1945
Japan is defeated at the end of World War II and withdraws from Beijing

1949
Mao Zedong declares the founding of the People's Republic of China, with Beijing as its capital

1958
Mao launches the Great Leap Forward in an effort to increase construction and manufacturing

1959-1961
A disastrous famine takes the lives of 30 million Chinese people

1965
A subway system opens in Beijing

1966
Mao Zedong launches the Cultural Revolution

1976
Mao Zedong dies in Beijing

1989
Troops fire on student demonstrators in Tiananmen Square

1993
Three beltways are completed around Beijing, and a new highway links the airport with the city center

BEIJING

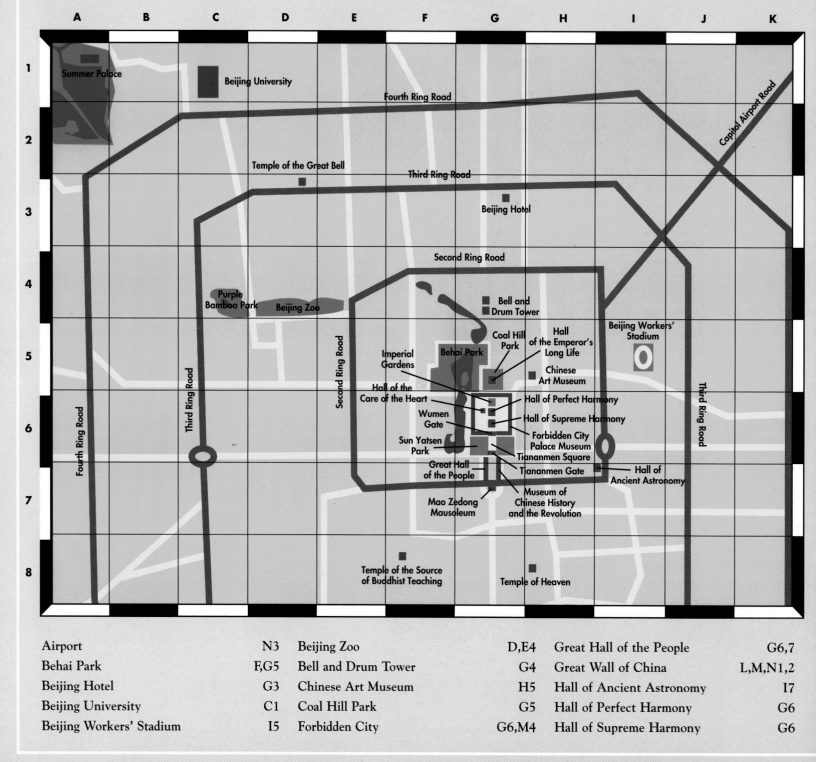

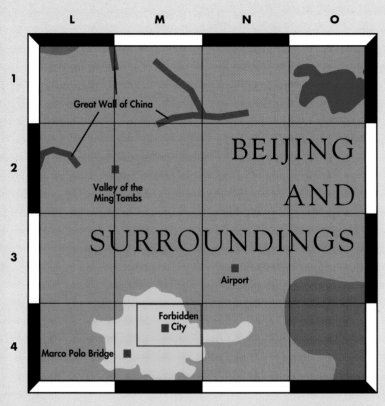

L M N O

BEIJING
AND
SURROUNDINGS

1
Great Wall of China

2
Valley of the
Ming Tombs

3
Airport

4
Forbidden
City

Marco Polo Bridge

GLOSSARY

appease: Satisfy with gifts or offerings

barbarian: Uncivilized foreigner

barricade: Protective wall

Buddhism: Asian religion that teaches that the soul lives many times on earth before it reaches its final reward

catastrophe: A widespread disaster

communism: Political system in which the state has nearly total power and personal profit is strictly limited

Confucianism: Chinese religion based on the idea that every member of society should fulfill his or her role in relation to others

cremate: To destroy by burning

Daoism: Chinese religion that stresses the harmony of human beings and nature

dynasty: Ruling family

faction: Small group following a political or military leader

imperial: Pertaining to an emperor or empress

intrigue: A secret plot

latrine: Outdoor toilet

moat: Water-filled ditch surrounding a palace or other structure, intended to discourage enemies

obscure: Little known

regal: Kingly, noble

treachery: Villainy, untrustworthy behavior

turret: Small watchtower

vagabond: Rootless wanderer, hobo

Picture Identifications

Cover: Bird kite; statue of a Mandarin guard on the Great Spirit Way to the Ming Tombs; the Gate of Heavenly Peace; two schoolgirls in Tiananmen Square
Title page: Chinese schoolchildren
Pages 4-5: The Gate of Heavenly Peace
Pages 8-9: Schoolchildren at an outdoor event
Pages 18-19: A section of the Great Wall of China
Pages 34-35: Beijing Opera singers in costume
Pages 46-47: The Marble Boat at the Summer Palace

Photo Credits:

Cover (bird kite), ©KK&A, Ltd.; cover (top right), ©Eugene G. Schulz; cover (background), ©Chromo Sohm/Sohm/**Unicorn Stock Photos;** cover (bottom), ©**Bonnie Kamin;** 1, ©M. Spector/**H. Armstrong Roberts;** 3, ©**KK&A, Ltd.;** 4-5, ©Kevin Morris/**Tony Stone Images, Inc.;** 6, ©**Photri, Inc.;** 7 (top), ©Steve Vidler/**SuperStock International, Inc.;** 7 (bottom), ©**Eugene G. Schulz;** 8-9, ©Paul Conklin/**Photo Edit;** 10 (left), ©L. S. Williams/**H. Armstrong Roberts;** 10 & 11 (sunflowers), ©**KK&A, Ltd.;** 11, ©**Photri, Inc.;** 12 (left), ©Yann Layma/**Tony Stone Images, Inc.;** 12 (right), ©Paul Grebliunas/**Tony Stone Images, Inc.;** 13 (top), ©Steve Cohen/**Dave G. Houser;** 13 (eggplant, squash, and gingerroot), ©**KK&A, Ltd.;** 14 (left), ©**Photri, Inc.;** 14 (right), ©Christopher Arnesen/**Tony Stone Images, Inc.;** 15, ©Yann Layma/**Tony Stone Images, Inc.;** 16 (top), ©Steve Vidler/**SuperStock International, Inc.;** 16 (bottom), ©Steve Cohen/**Dave G. Houser;** 17 (left), ©M. Koene/**H. Armstrong Roberts;** 17 (Buddha image), ©**KK&A, Ltd.;** 18-19, ©Russel Kriete/**Root Resources;** 19, **Corbis-Bettmann;** 20, Bibliotheque Nationale, Paris/**e.t. archive;** 21, Keren Su/**Tony Stone Images, Inc.;** 22, Bibliotheque Nationale, Paris/**e.t. archive;** 23 (left), **Stock Montage, Inc.;** 23 (right), ©**North Wind Pictures,** hand-colored engraving; 24 (left), National Palace Museum, Taiwan/**e.t. archive;** 24 (right), ©Joe Solem/**Photo Resources Hawaii;** 25 (top), **Bettmann;** 25 (bottom), **North Wind Picture Archives;** 26 (left), ©Steve Cohen/**Dave G. Houser;** 26 (right), ©**Photri, Inc.;** 27 (incense and incense burner), ©**KK&A, Ltd.;** 27 (right), ©K. Scholz/**H. Armstrong Roberts;** 28 (left), **The Bettmann Archive;** 28 (right), ©E. Duncan/**e.t. archive;** 29 (both pictures), **UPI/Bettmann;** 30 (left), ©Florent Flipper/**Unicorn Stock Photos;** 30 (right), ©**AP/Wide World Photos;** 31 (top), ©**Carl Purcell;** 31 (bottom), ©**AP/Wide World Photos;** 32 (left), UPI/Corbis-Bettmann; 32-33, ©Noboru Komine/**Photo Researchers, Inc.;** 33 (top), ©**AP/Wide World Photos;** 33 (center), ©**Photri, Inc.;** 34-35, ©George Holton/**Photo Researchers, Inc.;** 36 (top), ©Bachmann/**N E Stock Photo;** 36 (bottom), ©Keren Su/**Tony Stone Images, Inc.;** 37 (left), ©**Bonnie Kamin;** 37 (Ping-Pong paddle and Ping-Pong ball), ©**KK&A, Ltd.;** 38 (cricket cage), ©**KK&A, Ltd.;** 38 (right), ©Jeff Greenberg/**Photo Edit;** 39 (bird kite), ©**KK&A, Ltd.;** 39 (bottom), ©Russel Kriete/**Root Resources;** 40, ©Steve Vidler/**SuperStock International, Inc.;** 41 (left), ©**Eugene Schulz;** 41 (right), ©**Photri, Inc.;** 42 (New Year sign), ©**KK&A, Ltd.;** 42 (bottom left) & 43, ©Camerique/**H. Armstrong Roberts;** 44 (mooncakes), ©**KK&A, Ltd.;** 44 (bottom), ©**Photri, Inc.;** 45 (top), ©David F. Myers/**Tony Stone Images, Inc.;** 45 (bottom), ©Paul Chesley/**Tony Stone Images, Inc.;** 46-47, ©Russel Kriete/**Root Resources;** 48 (both pictures), ©**Photri, Inc.;** 49 (top), ©Steve Vidler/**SuperStock International, Inc.;** 49 (bottom), ©Diane Chun/**Photo Resource Hawaii;** 50 (top), ©Steve Vidler/**SuperStock International, Inc.;** 50 (bottom), ©Paul Chesley/**Tony Stone Images, Inc.;** 51 (left), ©Florent Flipper/**Unicorn Stock Photos;** 51 (right), ©Robert Everts/**Tony Stone Images, Inc.;** 52 (top), ©Noboru Komine/**Photo Researchers, Inc.;** 52 (bottom), ©Diane Chun/**Photo Research Hawaii;** 52-53, ©**Eugene G. Schulz;** 53 (top left), ©Steve Vidler/**SuperStock International, Inc.;** 53 (top right), ©Chromo Sohm/Sohm/**Photo Researchers, Inc.;** 54, ©**SuperStock International, Inc.;** 55 (top), ©M. Roessler/**H. Armstrong Roberts;** 55 (bottom), ©A. Tovy/**H. Armstrong Roberts;** 56 (left), ©Kevin Morris/**Tony Stone Images, Inc.;** 56 (right), ©C. Barr/**H. Armstrong Roberts;** 57 (left), ©Steve Vidler/**SuperStock International, Inc.;** 57 (middle), ©**Photri, Inc.;** 57 (right), ©M. Koene/**H. Armstrong Roberts;** 59, ©**Eugene G. Schulz;** 60 & 61, ©**KK&A, Ltd.**

INDEX

Page numbers in boldface type indicate illustrations

ABOUT THE AUTHOR

Deborah Kent grew up in Little Falls, New Jersey, and received her B.A. in English from Oberlin College. She earned an M.A. in Social Work from the Smith College of Social Work, and worked for several years at the University Settlement House in New York City. For five years she lived in San Miguel de Allende, Mexico, where she wrote her first novel for young adults. Deborah Kent is the author of a dozen young-adult novels as well as many titles in the Children's Press America the Beautiful series. She lives in Chicago with her husband and their daughter Janna.